Cozy Minimalist Home

More Style, Less Stuff

DEDICATION

Contents

Minimalist Living

Take a quick look around your living room and you'll notice that you have an endless barrage of stuff. Maybe you bought that stuff because you liked it. Maybe you received it as a gift. Maybe you saw it as potentially useful. But we as a nation have too much of it. In many cases, our giant piles of stuff cause us mental stress, can be physically taxing, and harm our environment. For many, the solution is to pursue a minimalist lifestyle.

1

But what exactly does it mean to live a minimalist life? In short, it means living with less. Not necessarily less money (you may actually find you have more at the end), but less possessions. It's about letting go of things you don't need, and actively deciding not to purchase more than what's necessary. While it's a tough adjustment (especially if you've collected a bit too much stuff), it can be a positive lifestyle change if you're looking to live a more sustainable, stress-free life.

Ready to start living a new way?

Find a Minimalist Living Method That Works for You

Minimalist lifestyles come in many different methods, so the first step in your journey to minimalism is finding the one that's right for you. Once you've scoped out the field and decided on the right method for you, it's time to start living the idea.

The Purge: Time to Rid Your Life of What You Don't Need

Before you can start minimalist living, you need to let go of what you don't need. That means it's time to declutter – possibly the hardest part of going minimalist. Go through your stuff, and using the method you've decided on, decide what's really necessary to keep (if the idea of doing it all at once seems terrifying, try a slow decluttering technique while starting to live out other minimalist principles). But in the interest of reducing waste, make sure that you're not just trashing all your unnecessary stuff: donate what you can, and if you have to dispose of specialty products like electronics, do it responsibly.

Replace the Shoddy Short-Term with Quality Long-Term

How many times over the past few years have you had to replace wardrobe basics like t-shirts and socks? What about kitchen items, like small appliances (of which you probably feel like you have way too many), or bedroom basics, like sheets and blankets? If you've had to replace them once (or more in the case of clothing), it might be time to start spending more to own less. Opting for high-quality, versatile pieces, like high thread count sheets in neutral colors, and multipurpose kitchen appliances like an Instant Pot or microwave oven, will feel like a big investment at first. But it pays off entirely when you realize that you have one appliance doing the work of five and sheets that will last you over a decade.

Integrate the Ultimate Minimalist Closet: a Capsule Wardrobe

Paring down your closet is a good way to reduce the amount of stuff in your home (and clear up more space), but a capsule wardrobe really takes it to the next level. Creating a capsule wardrobe involves reducing all the items in your closet to a set number of items (usually 20-30, or slightly more if including accessories) and wearing only those items in various combinations for a season. Each season involves switching out or adding a few additional pieces, but the general idea is to have a set of items that work together in a wide variety of combinations so you can focus less time on picking outfits and more time on what matters. It will reduce your stress levels, free up your time, and might even make you feel more put together.

5

Live Minimalist By Buying Less

You don't want to undo all the work you just did to make your home minimalist, but it's tempting to go right back to buying unnecessary items when they catch your eye. Training yourself to buy less is a slow, uphill battle, but practicing self-restraint is possible. Some easy ways to reduce your spending on stuff:

Go to experiences, like concerts and fairs, with friends instead of going on shopping trips

Set up daily texts from your bank letting you know what your account balance is — it will encourage you to keep saving and stop spending!

Only go shopping with a list (and stick to it)

Unsubscribe from emails from your favorite stores to avoid being tempted by sales

Say "No Thank You" to (Physical) Gifts

In all honesty, your loved ones probably would prefer giving you a gift they know you'll love, and getting those gifts will reduce the amount of stuff hindering you from living a minimalist lifestyle. So for your next birthday or holiday, ask your family and friends to skip any physical gifts. Instead, consider asking them to give money towards something you really want (like that trip to Spain you've been dreaming about), or set up a fundraiser online for a cause you care about in place of any gifts at all.

Sharing is Caring

It's tempting to buy something because you need it for a specific task, but for many items, you can crowdsource them instead. Utilize community groups like NextDoor and Buy Nothing to ask about borrowing specific items like garden or home tools instead of buying one you'll use once a year, or see if there's a tool library in your area to rent from. But sharing instead of buying extends beyond one-off items: your local library is a hub of books and media, and your area community center is an inexpensive and minimalist alternative to a home gym. Make use of them, and you'll not only own less, but get to know your neighborhood more.

Focus on the Important Stuff Instead of Just Physical Stuff

It's easy in a world that's constantly showing you ads for the newest products to get focused on what you own, but the key of minimalism is freeing up your time – and money – for the things that matter. Spending less time and money on stuff allows you the opportunity to learn more about issues you care about, connecting with others, and experiencing what's around you. Spend the time you save by going minimalist reconnecting with friends, exploring what's near you, and educating yourself on new topics and world news. Your physical and mental health will thank you.

Benefits of a Minimalist Home

Minimalism is countercultural. It is contrary to every advertisement we have ever seen because we live in a society that prides itself on the accumulation of possessions.

But there is more joy to be found in minimalist living than can be found pursuing more.

Benefits of Minimalism

Here are 21 powerful benefits of pursuing and living a minimalist lifestyle.

1. Spend Less.

One important benefit of minimal living is the simple reality that it costs less. As you accumulate fewer things, you spend less money. Additionally, it costs much less to store them, maintain them, repair them, clean them, and even discard them. And as your affection for physical possessions begins to fade, you'll find far more opportunity to use your finances in other ways.

Many people believe the secret to financial freedom is earning more money. Unfortunately, when we begin to make more money without spending restraints in place, we just spend more money... this truth has proven true over and over again (maybe even in your own life). Conversely, the reverse is probably more true: the secret to financial freedom is actually spending less. It's the simplest solution to (almost) all your money problems.

Live a life that accumulates only the essential often results in the financial freedom you've been searching for.

2. Less Stress.

A minimalist home is significantly less stressful. Being able to freely move around and enjoy your home is a huge weight off your shoulders.

Compare two counter tops: one that is clear (minimal) and one that is cluttered. Look at each of them separately and gauge your internal response. What exactly is your emotional and mental response? Notice how the clear countertop brings about a calming effect and the cluttered one bring emotions of distraction or anxiety. Now, magnify this emotional response throughout your entire home.

A minimalist home is significantly less stressful.

3. Easier to Clean.

The fewer things in our home, the fewer things there are to clean. This makes cleaning a significantly easier chore.

Clearly, the vast number of knick-knacks on the shelving made the proposition of dusting a daunting task. Additionally, when we finished decluttering our kids' toy room, we noticed it took much less time to put their toys away in the evening. And when we began decluttering our wardrobe, we found it easier to keep our closets tidy.

This benefit became very clear. The fewer things in our home, the easier it is to clean.

4. More Freedom.

The sense of freedom that comes from minimalism is truly refreshing. You will no longer feel tied to the material possessions in your home and you'll feel a new sense of independence.

5. Good for the Environment.

Assume for just a moment you have one of those mothers that does all the work around the house for you. Every morning when you wake up she makes your bed and the kitchen is spotless no matter what the family ate for dinner the night before.

If that was the case, how would you show the most respect and honor to your mother? Would you best bring her honor by pulling out every toy and making as large a mess as possible for her to clean? Or would you bring her honor by keeping things clean, by putting your own toys away, and keeping the room as close to perfection as possible? The second one of course. You would bring honor to her by sustaining the perfection that she desires for you as much as possible.

The less we consume and buy, the less damage we do to the environment.

6. Be More Productive.

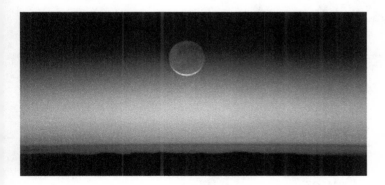

Our possessions consume our time more than we realize.

Take shopping for example: the average American spends nearly 12 hours every month shopping. Now, while it is impossible to completely remove shopping from our schedules, one benefit of living simply is the opportunity to live a more productive life by the plain fact that we spend less time shopping. Add in the time we spend cleaning, sorting, and organizing our stuff once we get it in our homes and we're beginning to talk about a significant chunk of time.

7. Example for my Kids.

These are valuable life lessons they will never learn in the media.

8. Support Other Causes.

Living a simple life provides the opportunity to financially support other causes. Minimalism provides an opportunity to not just save money for the sake of keeping it for myself, but to use it to further causes that I believe in.

Money is only as valuable as what we choose to spend it on.

9. Own Higher Quality Things.

Take your wardrobe for example: if you are like most, you have 25

mediocre shirts hanging in your closet – even though you really only wear 10 of them and truly love even less. A much more sensible approach is to have 10 shirts that you truly love hanging in your closet rather than 25 that you just "kinda like." Based on the budgetary reality that we only have a certain amount of money that we can spend on clothes, you can either purchase 20 shirts at $20 each or 10 at $40 each.

In this way, a minimalist lifestyle allows you to purchase higher quality items. Remember, more is not better… better is better.

10. Less Work for Someone Else.

In each case, someone other than the owner of the possessions was doing all the work. Consider the fact that at some point in your life (or in your death) every single item of your belongings will be sorted by another human being.

You can create for yourself a less stressful life today by living a minimalist life and lessen the burden on someone close to you as well. For the sake of your closest friends and family, choose to live a simple, minimalist life.

11. Be Happier.

Owning fewer possessions makes you happier.

According to a survey by the Simplicity Institute, an organization that surveyed 2,500 people across various countries who self-identified themselves as living with fewer possessions, 87 percent of respondents indicated they were happier now than when they owned more possessions.

Happiness is not found in owning as many possessions as possible; it's found living life consistent with your greatest passions.

12. Do Work You Love.

Confucius, an ancient Chinese philosopher, is credited with saying, "Choose a job you love, and you will never have to work a day in your life."

Whether you are 16, 26, or 76, you are making choices today that will chart the course for the rest of your life. And those who choose to embrace the idea of living with less open up the rest of his or her life to endless possibilities—including picking a passion as a career.

Somebody who decides to intentionally live with less has less need to hold a certain level of income. As a result, they can choose whatever career path they most desire. Their decision does not have to be dictated by income level. And while there is nothing wrong with earning money, when your salary package can be removed from the career-choice equation, you are free to choose your career based on other factors—such as "something I really want to do."

Own less stuff. Choose work you love.

13. Freedom From the Comparison Game.

Our culture begs us to own more. Advertisements call us to purchase the latest and the greatest. Our natural tendencies cause us to compare our lives with those around us. Add in the fact that we seem to have a built-in desire to impress others by owning as much as possible. And you've got a recipe for disaster.

As a result, we spend precious energy comparing our stuff to others. We spend so much mental energy thinking about what we don't own, we fail to appreciate the things that we do own. It makes us feel we are missing out on something—even though there is so much joy right in front of us.

14. Time for Things that Matter Most.

Every single thing you own requires a little bit of your attention and time whether it be researching, shopping, cleaning, organizing, repairing, replacing, recycling, or working just to make the money to buy the new thing that you can take home to clean and organize and replace.

That's why those who live a minimalist lifestyle have more time on their hands for other things in life. It was this benefit that ultimately led to our decision to become minimalists.

The more stuff you own, the more your stuff owns you.

15. Visually Appealing.

More appealing. Think about photos of homes that are cluttered, and photos of minimalist homes. The ones with almost nothing in them except some beautiful furniture, some nice artwork, and a very few pretty decorations, are the ones that appeal to most of us. The feeling is both calm and elegant. Things that value most are proudly on display. You can make your home more appealing by making it more minimalist.

16. Not Tied to the Past.

Clutter keeps you tied to the past. Your thoughts tend to dwell in the past as the things around you force your mind to reminisce. Solutions tend to be rooted in the past as the things around you conjure up the same old thought-processes. Additionally, our minds are tied to the past because there is no available space for anything new.

17. Less Places for Your Heart.

A wise teacher once said, "Where your treasure is, there your heart will be also." By that, he meant that our hearts will naturally gravitate to the things we have invested the most into.

One benefit of minimalism is that the less investment you put in material possessions, the less places your heart has to go. When we begin to invest our money, time, and lives into more meaningful things (like relationships, social causes, or raising our children), our hearts will be drawn to those things because that is where our life investment is going… and a white scrape in your maroon minivan won't ruin your entire day.

18. More Opportunity for Rest.

It is no coincidence that most of the major world religions exhort human beings to set aside time each week for rest. And even those who would not consider themselves religious still speak to the value of rest. As humans, we all have physical limitations.

There is a danger in our world to self-exalt ourselves over our limitations – to claim that we can work without rest. There is great danger in losing the natural rhythm between rest and work. Great danger for our physical bodies, our emotional well-being, our relationships, and our spirituality. Simply put, we must guard the natural rhythms of life.

Minimalism provides more opportunity for valuable rest, refreshment, and enjoyment. Removing the relentless pursuit of physical possessions from our lives frees us from the pursuit of the almighty dollar. Removing unnecessary physical possessions from our lives frees us from the burden of caring for them. Removing clutter from our

23

homes allows energy to flow more freely. And removing the value we place on physical items allows us to redirect our values and priorities.

So take a deep breath or better yet, take a nap. And return to the natural rhythms of work and rest.

19. Find Things Easier.

Own less clutter. Find stuff quicker.

20. Live in a Smaller Space.

According to statistics, the average house size in America has doubled since the 1950s—yet how many times have you heard someone complain their house is still too small? Chances are pretty good that our houses aren't too small

For most families, a house is the costliest investment they'll ever make—almost 40 percent of an average American's expenses go toward housing costs. Being able to live comfortably in a smaller home provides far more financial flexibility and stability.

21. Display What You Value Most.

Communicate what is most important. Minimalism isn't just the removal of all physical possessions. It is also the intentional promotion of the things I value most. It is about deciding what is most important in your life and removing the things that distract you from it.

One benefit of minimalism is that you are able to visibly declare what is most important to you. Look around your living room. What does it communicate about you? If a total stranger walked in, what would they identify is most important? Is it? Or has the most important things in your life become crowded out by less important things?

How to Create a Minimalist Home

Start Your Minimalist Home in the Living Room

Start your transition to a minimalist home with the room you visit most often—and that accumulates the most clutter. Start transitioning your living room to a minimalist style by first cleaning up the space and clearing off all the extra stuff you have lying around—on the coffee table, end tables, window ledges, and entertainment center. As you clean, don't just stick the random items in storage or reorganize them on the shelf. Dump your knick-knacks and magazines, and place loose papers where they belong (which might just be in the recycle bin).

Once you've cleared off your surfaces, you can focus on the furniture and statement pieces. Think about what you use in this space, and how you use it. Is your accent chair just a decorative piece? Does that end table just serve as a stand for a lamp you never use? When was the last time you lit the collection of candles sitting on the end table? If it's not functional, donate it. From here, you'll have to decide if you want to keep your current furniture or move to a more minimalist set of new furniture, like a sectional and coffee table instead of countless couches, chairs, and end tables.

With furniture figured out, there's one major piece of the living room remaining: decor. Any throw pillows and blankets you don't regularly use should be disposed of (you know you don't regularly use four throw pillows, so be brutal). While you're in the purging mood, nix any rugs. They're not entirely necessary decor, and getting rid of them will also allow you to get rid of any rug-cleaning products you have stashed away in the bathroom (but we'll get to that later).

Finally, it's time to look at the walls. Endless collections of framed family photos are cute in theory, but cluttered in reality. Opt to keep your walls minimalist by having two to three larger pieces of art on the walls, and keep one wall bare to balance the room. If you simply can't part with your photos and frames, at least rearrange them to form a gallery wall.

Go Minimalist in the Kitchen

Thinking logically, your kitchen is one of the most practical spaces in the home, so therefore, shouldn't it be the most inherently minimalist? While it's a nice idea, the truth is that most of our kitchens are weighed down with duplicate tools, overloaded pantries, and covered counters. You didn't pay for those nice marble countertops to hide them beneath cereal boxes, so if you're committed to minimalist living, the minimalist home has to include your kitchen.

Begin your transition to a minimalist kitchen by emptying out every cabinet and putting their contents on the counter and table (and if you really need space, the floor). Spot unnecessary duplicates? Expired pantry basics? Things you've forgotten you kept in the house? Donate them or throw them away.

With the first pass out of the way, it's time to get granular, starting with your kitchen utensils. Ditch duplicates of measuring cups, spoons, and other cooking utensils. And any utensils that are falling apart should go, too, but make a note to get new ones for yourself.

Which bring up an important point for establishing a permanent minimalist home, in your kitchen or elsewhere: buy quality items that will last in the long-term. Investing in quality kitchen utensils and supplies, like knives and cutting boards, will mean you need to buy less backups and duplicates, keeping your kitchen minimalist far beyond this first transition.

Once you've removed duplicates and beaten down items, it's time to consider the design of your kitchen. Open shelving or glass cabinetry lends itself well to stylish pieces and matching flatware sets. If you're lucky enough to have this in your kitchen, consider these exposed spaces a "functional display" area, and keep them minimally stocked. Doing so will also force you to purge more to make room in your other cabinets.

Next up, kitchen appliances. We all accumulate small appliances over time, from toasters to food processors to that blender from the year you were determined to drink smoothies more (we've all been there). Many of these are actually worth keeping in your kitchen (though if you've given up on smoothies, it's time to give up on the blender), but small appliances don't belong on your counter. You can keep one or two small appliances out—and make them the most used, like your coffee maker or toaster—but the rest should be stored away in closets or cabinets to be brought out when you need to use them (bonus: this will help you clear out more space, and force you to keep your appliances clean).

Which leads into the final, golden rule of maintaining a minimalist home in your kitchen: keep the counters clear. You don't need decorative salt shakers, knick knacks, or anything else cluttering them up. Think of your kitchen as a workspace, and minimalist design will come easily.

Minimalist Design Means Maximum Relaxation in Bedrooms

Let's talk about the space that should be the most minimalist, but probably is far from it: your bedroom. Minimalism in your bedroom can help keep you relaxed and create a haven from the day's work and activities. To make your bedroom space your more minimalist, follow one golden rule throughout, here more than anywhere else in the home: no excess anything.

et's start with one of the least minimal parts of your bedroom: your wardrobe. While developing a pared-down capsule wardrobe is a great step towards minimizing your wardrobe permanently, short-term minimizing can be done with a basic clothing purge. Once you've gotten rid of clothing you no longer wear, no longer like, or that no longer fits, all clothing belongs in your closet. Hang some of it, put a small wardrobe inside the closet it you have to, or stack it on the shelves. The point is, your clothing should be out of sight and stored all in one place so you're less inclined to leave it lying out across the room.

After you've tackled your closet, it's time to take some rules you learned when clearing out your living room and apply it to your bedroom, starting with pillows and blankets. If you have pillows and blankets on your bed that you don't use every day, get rid of them.

The same goes for all your bedroom decor. A lamp on your nightstand is fine if you use it, but a collection of framed family photos on your dresser is a no-go. Here, your decor should be functional or relaxing to fit the space's intention. Think candles, diffusers, and maybe a few favorite books–so long as it's not cluttered.

Bring the Minimalist Home to Your Bathroom

If you thought the room you visit to get clean would be inherently minimalist, you'd be wrong. The good news about minimizing your bathroom is that it's perhaps the easiest room to make minimal.

Decluttering your bathroom comes down to one thing that you probably have a lot of: products you no longer use. That half-empty bottle of color shampoo from when you had bleached hair. The moisturizer that didn't work out that well. The backup mascara for when your backup mascara runs out. Throw out any product you don't regularly use. Once you've winnowed down your product collection, winnow it down further in your shower to only products you use in the shower regularly (meaning at least every other day). Just like in the kitchen, store your items out of sight to appreciate your countertops and keep them clear.

Finally, there's bathroom decor to handle. If you guessed that such a high-function room should be devoid of decor, you're (mostly) right. A simple shower curtain (read: a single, muted color), a bath mat, and a trash bin are all you need to keep this room beautiful and functional.

Kiss Clutter Goodbye in Your Office

For those lucky enough to have an office space at home, you might have found it's both a blessing and a curse. As your "working" area at home, most of the things you don't want to deal with—bills, paperwork—end up there, making it cluttered and far from minimalist before you even get to your job-related items. Before you're ready to make your office the next room in your minimalist home, take some time to go through the unofficial "inbox" pile on your desk and deal with everything there.

Once that's done, it's time to find a permanent solution to the endless paperwork problem. A big file cabinet can be bulky and difficult to keep organized, so if you're willing to work digitally, buy a combination scanner/printer. These aren't much more expensive than basic printers, and will save you in the long run from mountains of clutter. Scan bills and other documents you want to hold onto, store them on your computer or an external hard drive, and toss out the paper copies.

Office supplies are another large source of clutter that make it difficult to maintain a minimalist home office. While it's tempting to buy these in bulk, most at-home offices don't require 1,000 packs of pencils or enough pen varieties to stock a small business. You probably own too much office supplies, so purge out the office supplies you don't use regularly (and the unnecessary backups).

You might notice that this leaves your desk cabinets and drawers feeling empty. This is a great place to put small things you can't scan or purge—a pile that is hopefully small at this point. If you don't have much you need to store, opt for a simpler desk without cabinets or storage. The few supplies you do need to keep can be put in a stylish desk organizer on top of the desk as a reminder to yourself not to buy things you don't have space for.

How to Declutter Your Home

Here are the top decluttering tips:

Do it in small chunks. Set aside just 15 minutes to declutter just one shelf, and when that shelf or that 15 minutes is up, celebrate your victory. Then tackle another shelf for 15 minutes the next day. Conquering an entire closet or room can be overwhelming, and you might put it off forever. If that's the case, just do it in baby steps.

Set aside a couple hours to do it. This may seem contradictory to the above tip … and it is. It's simply a different strategy, and I say do whatever works for you. Sometimes, for me, it's good to set aside part of a morning, or an entire Saturday morning, to declutter a closet or room. I do it all at once, and when I'm done, it feels awesome.

Take everything out of a shelf or drawer at once. Whichever of the two above strategies you choose, you should focus on one drawer or shelf at a time, and empty it completely. Then clean that shelf or drawer. Then, take the pile and sort it (see next tip), and put back just what you want to keep. Then tackle the next shelf or drawer.

Sort through your pile, one item at a time, and make quick decisions. Have a trash bag and a give-away box handy. When you pull everything out of a shelf or drawer, sort through the pile one at a time. Pick up an item, and make a decision: trash, give away, or keep. Don't put it back in the pile. Do this with the entire pile, and soon, you'll be done. If you keep sorting through the pile, and re-sorting, it'll take forever. Put back only what you want to keep, and arrange it nicely.

Be merciless. You may be a pack rat, but the truth is, you won't ever use most of the junk you've accumulated. If you haven't used it in the last year, get rid of it. It's as simple as that. If you've only used it once or twice in the last year, but know you won't use it in the next year, get rid of it. Toss it if it's unsalvageable, and give it away if someone else might be able to use it.

Papers? Be merciless, unless it's important. Magazines, catalogues, junk mail, bills more than a year old, notes to yourself, notes from others, old work stuff … toss it! The only exception is with tax-related stuff, which should be kept for seven years, and other important documents like warranties, birth and death and marriage certificates, insurance, wills, and other important documents like that. But you'll know those when you see 'em. Otherwise, toss!!!!

If you are on the fence with a lot of things, create a "maybe" box. If you can't bear to toss something because you might need it later, put it in the box, then close the box, label it, and put it in storage (garage, attic, closet), out of sight. Most likely, you'll never open that box again. If that's the case, pull it out after six months or a year, and toss it or give it away.

Create a system to stop clutter from accumulating. There's a reason you have tall stacks of papers all over the place, and big piles of toys and books and clothes. It's because you don't have a regular system to keep things in their place, and get rid of stuff you don't need. This is a topic for another day, but it's something to think about as you declutter. You'll never get to perfect, but if you think more intelligently about how your house got cluttered, perhaps you can find ways to stop it from happening again.

Celebrate when you're done! This is actually a general rule in life: always celebrate your accomplishments, no matter how small. Even if you just decluttered one drawer, that's great. Treat yourself to something delicious. Open that drawer (or closet, or whatever), and admire its simplicity. Breathe deeply and know that you have done a good thing. Bask in your peacefulness.

14 Things You'll Never Find in A Minimalist Home

Minimalism might be one of the most popular interior design trends at the moment, but it's also one of the most difficult to achieve.

Relying on simplicity and essentially outlawing the presence of lived-in details like clutter and mess (something that pretty tricky to stick to if you aren't a naturally tidy person), minimalism requires a certain level of commitment.

Which is why it can often be difficult to transition your home from one style of décor to minimalism. Before making the big jump, furniture needs to be re-purchased, unnecessary knick-knacks have to be thrown out, and you have to invest in clever storage opportunities so your laundry, kids' toys and exercise equipment are hidden from sight.

These stringent rules mean that there is now a list of things that you would never find in a minimalist home. From certain types of plants, to patterns on cushions, there are some standards no-nos in the Spartan décor world.

To assist you in your journey to complete minimalism, we've listed all the things you should think about getting rid of... or, at least, hiding in your closet.

1. Fussy Rugs

Moroccan or Persian style rugs; dated floral, check or striped patterns; or shaggy loomed styles tend to overpower spaces and draw the eye. Rugs in minimalist homes should aim to be unassuming, complementary and neutral in colour.

2. Flowering Plants

Although flowering plants are a sweet choice for garden beds and home entrances, they can look a little fussy when used as décor. Move shrubs and planters outside and replace with a more minimalist plant – like rubber plants or fiddle leaf figs. Even succulents are great for this.

3. Clashing Cushions

In minimalism, the aim of the game is cohesion. Your cushions don't have to match exactly, but having an overarching colour scheme or pattern helps keep them unified.

4. Exposed Knick-Knacks

While some artfully placed bits and bobs — like vases, books, and trinkets — can help your space feel more 'lived in,' it's best to keep most life accessories out of sight. Things like remotes, shopping bags and your exercise equipment should be tidied away after use.

5. Complex Patterns

Patterns in small doses, or blown out to be oversized, can definitely work in minimalist spaces. However, overly busy, tight or complex patterns should be avoided as they overcomplicate the space.

This one might not be as obvious, but you also won't see a lot of floral patterns in a minimalist home. Floral patterned chairs, sofas, wallpaper or other room features dates the space easily, and draws the eye unnecessarily.

6. All-Over Carpet

Although it's not always under your control, the minimalist style lends itself better to clean wood or tiled flooring. Dated carpet choices in white, beige or greys can be harder to style.

7. Clutter

It goes without saying but general clutter doesn't really have a place in minimalism. Stacks of magazines, chewing gum packs, old coffee mugs, and wrappers muddle the area.

Disposable items like coffee cups, takeaway containers, water bottles and other plastic things, should live in the cupboard or the bin.

8. Too Many Colours

When decorating, the easiest and most straight-forward way to do is to build a neutral base and then introduce some soft, complementary colours like deep blues, forest greens or blush pinks. However, when you have too many competing colours in one place it can convolute the design.

9. Defunct Décor

Items in your house that no longer serve a purpose and don't fit in with your style – for example, your spouse's sports memorabilia, that hat stand you don't use, and that vase of fake flowers – should be removed and replaced with useful and chic alternatives.

10. Household Products

Although we need them, household products like cleaning sprays, dishrags, laundry detergent, and dishwasher liquid, should be kept out of sight to keep things orderly.

11. Exposed Wires, Cables Or Phone Lines

When styling your home, employ some clever tricks to make sure your TV's cords, your phone wires and your charges aren't cluttering your space.

12. Unnecessary Kitchen Accessories

Barbecue tongs, egg timers, avocado slicers, measuring cups and apple corers are all very useful items, but for the sake of minimalism, should be kept in drawers and cupboards, and not on benches.

13. Busy Or Chintzy Furniture

As a general rule, the furniture found in minimalist homes is sleek, functional, streamlined and un-fussy. Over-stuffed couches, dated carved tables and oversized chairs tend to over-complicate things.

14. Distracting Bright Colours

There's no reason to shy away from a pop of colour in your minimalist home, if that's what you want. However, if the presence of the colour is too jarring or distracting, it's a good idea to relax it to a softer shade. We would suggest staying away from overpowering colours of the neon variety.